Adjusting Your Practice

Strategies for building a successful chiropractic clinic

By Mike Cameron, D.C.

To my loving daughter, Aria. Without whom I would be wandering lost in the dark.

What now?

So you just dedicated the better part of a decade taking classes that most people can't even pronounce, let alone comprehend, questioning why you pay rent for an apartment because you spend all your time at the library, and contemplating whether or not you should start buying stock in the energy drinks that fueled your all night study sessions for the board exams; congratulations, now comes the hard part.

When I first started into practice. I quickly realized that there is a pretty steep learning curve when it comes to owning a business, and for some of my colleagues it was too steep. The whole point of this book is to supplement your education with modern techniques and strategies that will make your clinic a viable entity in today's economy.

Start from the beginning.

Hopefully by the time you have graduated, you will know what state you will want to practice in. A useful website is the Federation of Chiropractic Licensing Boards: www.fclb.org. The site contains licensing requirements, definition of scopes of practice, and even continuing education requirements by state. Each state is different so make sure you know what you are getting in to before you set up shop.

Once you have decided on the state, the next step is to apply for your license. For most states, you need to submit an application (with a fee); along with transcripts from your undergrad/chiropractic schools, as well as proof that you passed the required board exams.

After you apply for your state license, you can start narrowing down what region you want to practice in. Back in the day, all you had to do is hang your shingle, and your business will prosper. Nowadays you have to be smarter with your location. When looking for a city, I would focus on the chiropractor to population ratio (1 chiropractor to every 10,000 people in the city makes starting a new practice much easier). Obviously, the more saturated the chiropractic market is in the area; the harder it will be to get new patients.

Now that you have the city picked out, you should be putting some thought into the name of the clinic. This is one of the most important steps you will do because this will be your brand, and it will represent you for your entire career. The name of your clinic will be on a lot of paperwork, so it will be ridiculously tedious if you decide to change it down the road. Most chiropractors choose to just have their last name i.e. "Smith Chiropractic Clinic". Personally, I named my clinic after the city that I'm in. I feel that not only does it give the clinic a sense of permanence, but it also conveys the fact that you are loyal to the city, which a surprisingly large number of my patients appreciate.

So now we have our location, and clinic name. The next step is to find a physical address. There are lots of options for this part, depending on what you want your clinic to be. Some choose to rent out space, others want to buy a building, and others embed their clinic in another business like a medical office or physical therapy clinic. Your tastes may change over the years, or hopefully your clinic will grow to the point where you need a larger space. While it is favorable that you stay in one place, don't feel like you are going to be tied down at the same location for the next 30 years. I rented space for 5 years, and then my clinic grew to the point where I purchased a larger building a block away, and 5 years after that, I relocated to a more modern building with much more parking (which I needed due to patient growth).

No matter where you decide to work, chances are that you will need to do some improvements/build out to the space (especially if you will use X-Ray). This means that you will have about a month or so of downtime. During this time, you should already have your license, so now you can apply for your National Provider Identification (NPI) number. This is a fairly simple process. You need to go to https://nppes.cms.hhs.gov/, create an account, and fill out an application. However, you will need your license number, and preferably your practice location address. You will need to apply for an individual and a group NPI number. The final step is to get a tax identification number (TIN). For this, go to www.irs.gov, or you can call their toll free number: 800-829-4933, and you should be able to receive your number at the end of the call. The final step in forming your business is, simply put, to make sure your butt is protected. There are a lot of malpractice companies/plans out there so make sure to choose which one best suits your needs. There are two basic types of medical malpractice insurance: claims made and occurrence. The main difference between the two is their willingness to accept liability if coverage is terminated. For example, say you have an occurrence policy for a year, and then cancelled it because you won the lottery and retired. If a patient that you saw during that year decided to sue you, the occurrence policy will cover it. However, if you had a claims made policy in that situation, you would be liable for any damages because you do not currently have an active policy. The other aspect of malpractice insurance you need to be concerned with is the policy limit per claim and per year. I've seen policies that covered over one million dollars per claim, and up to three million dollars per year. While these limits will certainly protect you from paying anything out of pocket, the reality of the situation is that as long as the doctor does not intentionally hurt a patient, and they can prove that the therapy performed was reasonable and customary for the diagnosis, and then it will not be a million dollar settlement. I've seen chiropractor's accidently break a rib on a patient, and the claim was settled out of court for around $20,000 plus legal/medical fees. Having said that, it is very realistic to have a policy with only $100,000 per claim and up to $300,000 per year. The lower the limits, the more affordable the insurance plan will be, and, at least in the beginning of your business, every dollar counts. Another aspect of protection for a new business owner is becoming incorporated. This will provide another barrier from a patient suing the doctor for their personal assets. The two main options for becoming incorporated are either to become a professional corporation (PC), or a limited liability company (LLC). Both can protect the individual business owner from having their personal assets seized, but they differ by how the business is taxed. A PC can either be a S-Corp or a C-Corp. In a S-Corp, the profits/losses are reported to the government and any profit that is made by the business is taxed. In a C-Corp, the business files a corporate tax return, paying tax on any profits, and the business owner will also get taxed on any profits that they receive. A LLC is similar to a S-Corp in that the business is only taxed once; however a LLC is a lot more flexible in terms of how a business is managed. There are also a lot less compliance issues associated with an LLC, such as no need for a board of directors or annual meetings, and far less record keeping has to be done. It would be wise to sit down with an attorney that specializes in becoming incorporated for this step. The fee that you have to pay for their service could be insignificant compared to the amount you could potentially overpay if you decide the wrong path for your business.

Can I finally practice now?!

Well it may have taken a few months, but at this point you should have your license, your NPI numbers, your TIN, as well as a business name/location. However, these steps just enabled you to legally practice. You still need to figure out what type of practice you even want to have (starting to see how complicated this can be?). The clinic with the lowest stress is usually 100% cash based, however, in our current economy that is virtually impossible. I do know several colleagues that started out as all cash, but when they finally decided to take insurance, their business grew significantly.

Insurance 101.

If you decide that an all cash practice is what you want, then feel free to skip this section. However, if you want to actually make any money with your clinic, I would read on. There are several components of every insurance plan that you need to know. First is the deductible. This is just the amount that a patient needs to pay themselves before their benefits kick in. I have seen patients who thought they had good insurance, but they had a $10,000 deductible, and none of it had been met. When this occurs, the patient usually opts to just be a cash patient (it turns out to be cheaper in the long run). The next component is copay/coinsurance. A copay is a set amount that a patient will have to pay each visit (after the deductible has been satisfied). A coinsurance is a percentage (usually 10% or 20%) that a patient needs to pay. At this time it is important to point out that most insurance companies do not pay 100% of what you bill. For example, if you bill

$45 for an adjustment, the insurance may only approve $40, which means the coinsurance will be a percentage of the approved amount (a 10% coinsurance with an approved amount of $40 would be $4 per visit). It is important to look up the approved amounts for each insurance company (called fee schedules), so that you are able to bill what is customary in the area. The final aspect of an insurance plan you should pay attention to is the visit limitations. This is pretty self-explanatory; just the amount of visits that are allowed per contract period.

If you decide to go into the insurance game, you will need to get a CAQH number (Council for Affordable Quality Healthcare). Their website is http://www.caqh.org/. The whole point of a CAQH number is to save you time when applying to different insurance companies. Years ago, you had to fill in the same information over and over again for each insurance company you apply to. Now, all you need to do is fill out the information once, get issued a CAQH number, and just provide the number on the insurance application.

As for which insurances to take, that is completely up to you. I will suggest to try and be in network with as many Preferred Provider Organization (PPO) insurances as you can, and stay away from Health Maintenance Organization (HMO) insurances. This is because most HMOs require a referral from the patient's primary care doctor, which can be like pulling teeth at times. Enrolling in Medicaid is as simple as going online and searching for your states Medicaid website. Provider applications for commercial insurances are usually fairly easy to find. Just go to their website, find the provider section, and look for links to enroll as a new provider. Medicare is a bit more complicated. The website to enroll in Medicare is https://pecos.cms.hhs.gov (makes sense right?) The Medicare website (medicare.gov) is aimed at patients, and you will just spend hours being frustrated if you start there. No matter if you decide to be in network or not with Medicare, you legally need to enroll and obtain your Medicare number. On average, the process of enrolling in a network can take up to 60 days. Some insurances will let you retroactively bill (bill for a past date) during the process, but they will rarely pay for a visit that occurred before you started the enrollment process. To keep things simple, I would be in network with your desired insurance companies before you treat your first patient.

Alright, alright now can I start practicing?!

Hahahahaha……..no. You have your location, and are now allowed to bill insurances, but you have to figure out how you are going to send out the billing (did I mention the process of opening your own clinic can be difficult). At its core, billing is broken down into Common Procedure Terminology (CPT), and International Classification of Disease (ICD) codes. ICD codes are the diagnosis that you gave a patient, and CPT codes are what you did to treat that specific diagnosis. Your ICD and CPT codes have to make sense with each other. For example, you cannot diagnose someone with hip dysplasia, then bill for a spinal adjustment. The claim will be denied because you diagnosed a problem with the hip region, but you only applied treatment to the spine. For this example, the correct way to bill would be to also diagnose a lumbar/sacral dysfunction (which they will almost always have) along with the hip dysplasia, then you will be able to bill for the spinal adjustment. You would also be able to bill for an extra spinal adjustment, however, claims with extra spinal adjustments usually require the doctor to send in specific medical documentation along with the claim (each insurance has different policies on this, and they often change). Chiropractic CPT and ICD-10 (10 is the current version) codes can easily be found online.

Now that you have some background on billing, you need to decide if you want to do it yourself, or hire a biller. THERE IS NO REASON TO HAVE A MEDICAL BILLER. There are lots of electronic medical record programs out there, and almost all of them allow you to submit your insurance claims electronically with just a click of a button. I'm not getting any money for this endorsement, but my clinic has been using ChiroFusion for years, and it is very easy to use, and low cost. Whatever you decide, I would opt for one that is cloud based, so that you   wont be tied to a single computer if you need to schedule (because patients will often contact you during non-business hours looking for an appointment.).

If you decide to do your own billing (which you should do), you will also need to find a clearinghouse. These act as intermediaries between you and the insurance companies. You send a file to them that contains visit information from patients with different insurances, and the clearinghouse sorts the visits, and delivers the bill to the appropriate insurance company. Whatever program you use will often have a list of clearinghouses that they recommend as well as how to sign up for them. They all are the same, so just pick the one that is the cheapest.

OK, I'm finally open! Where is everyone?

So you spent the last several months filling out so much paperwork that your paper cuts have paper cuts, and now you are finally ready to reap the rewards. However, when you open your doors on that first day, hardly anyone comes in. What the hell?! Doesn't everyone know how awesome your adjusting skills are, and how much chiropractic can benefit their life? Oh wait, they don't because you haven't done anything to get you name out to the public. Now up to this point, the book has given you facts about where to get the myriad of things you need for a business. The rest of the book will be my opinion on what needs to be done in order to have a successful practice. Some of these details you may think may be too small to even matter, but here is one last fact for you: according to the Bureau of Labor and Statistics, only about half of new businesses survive the initial five years. Got your attention? I hope so.

One thing you will quickly realize when you open your doors, is that you will become a target for parasitic marketing companies. It doesn't matter what their medium is, never pay a company to market or advertise for you. No company will guarantee (in writing) that your business will grow from using them. I purchased a 20 year old clinic that was losing $50,000 per year, and he was using a practice management company. The first thing I did was cancel their contract, and now, sixteen years later, my clinic is making well into six figures. So believe me when I say it is very possible. As a new business, you have to walk that fine line of trying to get your name out there, without going broke. Personally, I do not advertise at all, but there are 2 marketing items that I pay for: business cards, and the clinic's website. Now there are many places online that you can buy business cards from that are relatively cheap. When making a business card, just remember to be concise. Your clinic's name, address, phone, fax, and maybe e-mail along with your name and title should be the only thing on the card. If you put too much information on it, the card would look cluttered and unprofessional. I splurge and get the cards with spaces on the back to write in the patient's appointment times, and even with that I only spend about $150.00 a year on them. Now for the website, there are many business that will make one for you (at a huge cost), then charge you a monthly maintenance fee. What they don't want you to know is that you do not have to be a web developer in order to make a decent website.

There are numerous websites where you can build your own site from pre-made templates, and even purchase your domain through them. There is a monthly fee to use their service, but it is very minimal. Most of those sites are very user friendly, and usually all you have to do is click and drag to add whatever text or picture you would like. For my website, I pay $140 a year, and that includes the $20 a year you have to spend on renewing your domain. So in total, I spend less than $300.00 a year on marketing, and absolutely nothing on advertising, and manage to see about 30 new patients a month, on average. What's the secret? I do spinal screening at various stores and festivals…..just kidding. As a brief side note: NEVER become so desperate that you start doing spinal screenings at public events like an old-timey snake oil salesman. Chiropractic has made considerable advancements in public opinion over the last several decades, yet there are some of the general public are still skeptic. If you want to be treated like a medical professional, act like one. Do you ever see medical doctors with booths trying to persuade people to come and see them? No. That's because they believe that their profession is one that can benefit society, and that as long as they properly do their job, they will be successful. You need to adopt that same mentality.

There are three main avenues I use to get my name out: myself, the internet, and patients. What I do is actually pretty simple. I go out to lunch or dinner in the city that my clinic is in. I always try to go somewhere different, and if the place isn't overly busy, I'll talk to manager/owner after I'm done eating and compliment the establishment. When I'm done, I'll simply hand them my card, and say something like "Hopefully you'll never need this, but if you do feel free to give me a call". That's it. No pitch, no pressure, just walk away. A fellow business owner will appreciate the compliment, and respect that fact that you didn't try to market to them. But wait a minute, you just made them aware of your clinic, and now they have a positive connotation with it and you....you DID just market to them....sneaky. Whenever possible, utilize this strategy for any service you might need: haircuts, car repair, even if you are out have a few drinks with some friends. It doesn't cost anything to be nice, and besides, you get to write off each excursion as a business expense on your taxes.

Next, the internet. There is a concept called search engine optimization (SEO) that you need to be familiar with. Simply put, the more traffic that a website gets, the higher it is to the top when someone searches for you. Remember when I recommend that you name your clinic after the city you practice in? SEO is another reason to do that. People will rarely search for "Bob Smith, chiropractor", but they will often type "chiropractor" along with their cities name in order to find one close to them. If your clinic has the cities name in it, then the search engine will think that the person was looking for you specifically, and put your listing close to the top. Next, add your clinic's information to various business listing search programs (Yellow Pages, Yelp, etc.). Always make sure that you put your websites link down on those sites. I have a massage therapist, and when I first started out I decided to help her out as well as boost my clinics online rating at the same time. So I utilized an online discount business (like Groupon). In general, these types of businesses can hurt you because they cater to the bargain hunters, which provides no repeat business. However, it was good at giving my massage therapist some money up front, and when the deal ran, I made sure the website of the clinic was listed on it. In the 24 hours that the deal was up, my clinic's site received over 1,000 hits. Since then, I have been at the top of the major search engines when someone searches for a chiropractor in the city that I practice in.

Lastly, the patient. Patient referrals should make up the bulk of the new patients that come to your clinic. If it doesn't, then you need to change things immediately because this is the most crucial factor that determines if your clinic will prosper. My philosophy when it comes to patients has always been to offer as many therapies as I can in order to efficiently reduce their pain and correct their problem, don't charge an arm and a leg for it, and finally, don't be a dick (that last one can be hard sometimes). The majority of chiropractors in my area are straight rack 'em, crack 'em. They don't offer any type of pretreatment before the adjustment, or therapy after. Everyone has their own tastes, and feel free to practice how you see fit, but the typical patient visit at my clinic is as follows: patient lays prone on an automated flexion/distract table with heat (hydrocollator) to the affected area for about 15 minutes, then they get adjusted, and after the adjustment, they get another 15 minutes on a roller table with interferential therapy applied at the same time. If it is a new patient, I also educate them on how the problem occurred, steps that they can take to prevent the same thing from happening in the future, and I send them home with some samples of Biofreeze (you can request samples from their website) along with a stretch or two to perform at home. Each visit takes a little over 30 minutes. I have two adjusting rooms, and one therapy room, so I can have three patients going at the same time. For most commercial insurances, you will get paid for everything except the hot pack, which means you don't have to rely on treating over 100 patients a day. In the beginning, focus on getting more money per visit, and not more visits per day. The more visits per day will come when your appreciative patients tell their family and friends about the great new chiropractor in town that thoroughly treats your problem, instead of just cracking your back and kicking you out to make room for the next patient. This ideology should be at the heart of your clinic, and it is so important that I'm going to put it in bold. **Take care of your patients as much as you can, and they will take care of you.** I recently treated a patient that found me online, and was so grateful, that within the next month she had referred eleven of her friends and family members to me. The hope is that all patients will be satisfied to the extent that they refer you to others, so treat all patients with the care and respect they deserve. You don't get to have off days, or days where you are grumpy. The patient is paying to get your best, and if you do not deliver, then you are doing them a disservice. If you decide to take commercial insurance, every once in a while they will send you a performance summary to see how you compare to the other chiropractors in your area (your competition). This is a very useful tool because you

will be able to see what is lacking in your clinic. Since I offer as many services and therapies as possible, there is no need to try and sell the patient with a heavy handed sales approach. They appreciated the time and effort that I put into their care, which, in turn, lead to them referring in others. To this day, my number of services and therapies is still the same as when I started. The only thing that is different now is that my number of monthly patient visits are usually over double what the average is in the area.

The importance of first impressions.

The therapy offered and bedside manner delivered are the main factors that contribute to patient satisfaction, however, there are other things to consider that contribute as well. I always look at a new patient visit like going on a first date. You only have a finite amount of time to make a good first impression, so I make sure to cover all the senses. I can still distinctly remember from the early days of my clinic when a patient brought in her six year old son, and as soon as he stepped through the door he looked at his mom and said "This place smells like grandmas nursing home". Now if you clean and disinfect your clinic (and tables) regularly, it is hard to avoid that sterile medical smell. However, it's really simple to add an oil diffusor or even a plug in scent releaser to cover it up. I even go so far as to change the scent with the seasons: apple and cinnamon for fall, vanilla for winter, cherry blossom for spring, and some sort of citrus for summer. Think that is a bit excessive? I don't know, it may be. Then again, I was too busy trying to do everything thing that I can to avoid being in that half that fails within the first five years. At least once a month, I'll have a patient comment on how nice the clinic smells, which beats the hell out of them thinking that it smells like a nursing home. For sound, I play music over Bluetooth speakers spread throughout the clinic that are connected to my work laptop. Utilize whatever music service you want, just make sure that the play list is ad free (you don't want a massage to get interrupted by a car insurance commercial).

Finally, the visual aspect. For this, being cheap simply will not do. Spend the extra money and get comfortable leather chairs for your reception area. I've seen new clinics who tried to save money and used metal folding chairs. Not only does it look unprofessional, it makes you seem desperate for business. There isn't a lot, but the internet has some chiropractic art that you can use. I had a large blank wall that I wanted to fill, but couldn't find anything so I hired a local artist to paint something. Patients always comment on the painting, not only because of its scale (it's about 10ft x 4ft), but because it's an original piece by a local artist.

Don't just hang inspirational quotes all over your clinic, make your art visually appealing. Every clinic should be clean, so I won't waste time telling you to vacuum or empty the garbage. However, make sure your clinic is orderly. A front desk that's cluttered with papers looks disorganized, and can convey a sense of incompetence. Even the rooms need to be almost minimalistic. Each adjustment room of mine only contains the table, a chair, and a storage cabinet. Too much furniture can make the room seem crowded. Again, did I overthink this aspect? Ask the other half of the businesses that closed if their problem was that they spent *too* much time thinking about their business.

Common pitfalls of a new business.

In the time since I opened my doors, I have seen several dozen other business around me close. Each time it was for similar reasons. The owner did not have enough startup capital, their prices were too high for the product, or their service was lackluster (or a combination of all three). Every single failed owner that I had talked to always blamed something besides themselves. This is YOUR business, YOU control it, and YOU alone are responsible for it. There will be times when something out of your control screws up, and as much as you want to place a blame on someone else, you need to remain professional and accept responsibility.

I mentioned before that lack of startup capital can be a huge problem. It doesn't matter if you get a bank loan, or a private investor for the initial build out and decorating costs, chances are pretty fair that you will need to supplement your income in the first couple of years. Chiropractors receive an extensive education in the sciences, so use it to your advantage. Most local colleges have openings in the basic or health science departments. Personally, I taught Anatomy and Physiology for the first couple of years, and there were times that I was really glad that I had that additional income. On top of that, telling your patients that you are also a college professor makes you seem that much more credible and trustworthy. If you decide to pursue an additional job in the beginning, just make sure that it does not hinder your professionalism. A colleague of mine took a side job at an upscale wine store. He thought it was great (hey discounted wine), until one of his patients walked in. Not only did that patient never return to his clinic, but you can bet that the patient told others about the experience, which hurts our professional overall. When you graduate, even though you are a new doctor, you are still a doctor and are held at higher standards. Do not shoot yourself in the foot just to make a few extra bucks (or a bottle of wine).

I know this was a lot to take in – especially since your brains are probably mush right now from trying to pass your board exams. So here's a general breakdown of common problems (as well as ways to fix or avoid them):

1. Undercapitalization and Cash Flow Miscalculations

One of the most common reasons new clinics fail is simple: they run out of money.

Many new chiropractors underestimate startup costs and overestimate early revenue. Lease deposits, build-out expenses, equipment purchases (adjusting tables, digital X-ray units, EHR systems), credentialing fees, insurance, marketing, and staffing costs add up quickly. Even modest clinics can require $75,000–$250,000+ in startup capital depending on location and scope of services.

The bigger issue, however, is cash flow. Insurance reimbursement cycles can take 30–90 days. If you are credentialing with payers, it may take months before you can bill at all. Meanwhile, rent, utilities, payroll, malpractice insurance, and loan payments are due immediately.

Common mistakes:

- Assuming patients will come immediately.
- Not having 6–12 months of operating reserves.
- Taking out too much high-interest debt.
- Failing to project conservative revenue estimates.

Solution: Build a detailed 12-month cash flow forecast. Assume lower-than-expected patient volume for the first 3–6 months. Maintain a financial cushion.

2. Poor Location Selection

Location can make or break a new clinic. A beautiful office in a low-traffic industrial zone will struggle, while a modest office in a high-visibility retail corridor may thrive.

Key factors often overlooked:

- Demographics (age distribution, income levels).
- Competition density.
- Parking availability.
- Visibility from main roads.
- Accessibility for elderly or disabled patients.

Some new chiropractors choose locations based solely on cheap rent. Low rent often correlates with low foot traffic.

Solution: Conduct demographic research, traffic counts, and competitive analysis before signing a lease. Speak with neighboring businesses. Visit the area at different times of day.

3. Inadequate Marketing Strategy

"Build it and they will come" does not apply to healthcare.

Many chiropractors open their doors assuming referrals will organically flow. In reality, without a marketing plan, growth is slow and inconsistent.

Common marketing pitfalls:

- No defined target patient population.
- Overreliance on social media without strategy.
- Ignoring Google Business optimization.
- No community engagement.
- No referral relationship development with local providers.

Effective clinics often combine:

- Local SEO.
- Community events.
- Referral networking.
- Patient education workshops.
- Reputation management (online reviews).

Solution: Develop a written 6–12 month marketing plan before opening. Allocate a specific monthly marketing budget.

4. Credentialing and Insurance Billing Errors

Credentialing delays are a frequent early setback. It can take 60–180 days to be approved by major insurers. If you open before being credentialed, you may be limited to cash-pay patients.

Billing mistakes can also cripple revenue:

- Incorrect coding.
- Poor documentation.

- Lack of compliance with payer guidelines.
- Failure to track denials.

Denied claims create revenue leaks that many new clinics fail to monitor.

Solution: Start credentialing 4–6 months before opening. Consider hiring an experienced billing professional or service. Ensure documentation supports medical necessity.

5. Weak Business Systems

Clinical skill does not automatically translate to business competence.

Common operational gaps include:

- No standardized intake process.
- No financial policy enforcement.
- Inconsistent scheduling protocols.
- Poor follow-up systems.
- No KPIs (Key Performance Indicators).

Without systems, growth leads to chaos rather than scalability.

Solution: Develop written protocols for:

- New patient onboarding.
- Re-exams and care plans.
- Collections and payment policies.
- Appointment reminders.
- Staff roles and responsibilities.

Track KPIs such as visit average, patient acquisition cost, collections percentage, and cancellation rates.

6. Hiring Too Soon—or Too Late

Staffing missteps are common.

Hiring too early drains capital. Hiring too late causes burnout and poor patient experience.

Additionally, many chiropractors hire based on personality alone without defining clear job expectations. This leads to performance issues and turnover.

Solution:

- Clearly define job descriptions.
- Cross-train staff.
- Start lean but plan staffing milestones tied to patient volume.

7. Overexpansion of Services Too Quickly

New clinics often attempt to offer everything immediately:

- Massage therapy.
- Functional medicine.
- Decompression therapy.
- Neuropathy programs.
- Supplements.
- Digital X-ray.
- Shockwave therapy.

While diversification can increase revenue, premature expansion increases overhead and complexity.

Solution: Establish a stable core service model first. Add services only when patient volume and cash flow justify expansion.

8. Regulatory and Compliance Oversights

Healthcare is highly regulated. Failing to comply with federal and state regulations can result in fines or legal action.

Areas commonly overlooked:

- HIPAA compliance.
- OSHA requirements.
- Proper documentation standards.
- Advertising compliance.
- Fee-splitting laws.
- Anti-kickback statutes.

Even social media claims about "curing" conditions can trigger scrutiny.

Solution: Consult with a healthcare attorney during setup. Maintain compliance training for staff. Perform regular documentation audits.

9. Lack of Clear Vision and Brand Identity

Many new clinics fail to define:

- Who they serve.
- What differentiates them.
- Their treatment philosophy.
- Their brand voice.

Without clarity, marketing becomes generic and forgettable.

Are you:

- A family wellness clinic?
- A sports performance clinic?

- A pain-focused rehab clinic?
- A corrective care specialty office?

Solution: Define your niche early. Align your branding, messaging, and services around that identity.

10. Burnout and Poor Work-Life Boundaries

Opening a clinic often requires long hours, stress, and financial pressure. Many chiropractors work:

- Full clinic days.
- Evenings doing billing.
- Weekends marketing.
- Constant administrative tasks.

Without boundaries, burnout happens quickly.

Burnout leads to:

- Poor patient interaction.
- Reduced clinical quality.
- Decision fatigue.
- Emotional exhaustion.

Solution:

- Build structured office hours.
- Delegate early.
- Protect personal time.
- Develop mentorship support networks.

11. Unrealistic Patient Retention Expectations

Some new owners assume patients will commit to long-term care immediately. In reality, trust must be built.

Common retention mistakes:

- Overloading patients with long care plans without education.
- Poor communication of value.
- Failing to explain treatment goals.
- Not setting clear expectations.

Retention is built through:

- Education.
- Clear communication.
- Measurable outcomes.
- Strong patient relationships.

12. Ignoring Data and Metrics

Running a clinic without tracking numbers is like adjusting blindfolded.

Critical metrics include:

- New patients per month.
- Conversion rate.
- Visit average.
- Collections percentage.
- Overhead percentage.
- Patient acquisition cost.

Without these metrics, problems go unnoticed until cash flow suffers.

Solution: Review financial and operational metrics monthly. Make data-driven adjustments.

This is a hell of a lot of work. Is it worth it?

In the beginning, you will find yourself lying awake at night asking yourself this same question over and over. It is important to keep reminding yourself why you decided to go into chiropractic in the first place. Our branch of alternative medicine is truly awesome to be involved in. Over the years, I have helped countless patients overcome their problems and return to a normal life. Some were even contemplating suicide because the pain was unbearable, and traditional medicine had nothing to offer except medication. We wield a miraculous power, so as long as you maintain your professionalism, and always do right by your patients I guarantee that you will not only have a successful clinic, but will have a tremendous impact on the lives of people in your community. When you have the ambition to help others, and dedicate your life to that purpose, there is no limit to the heights that you can reach.